AF390680

Comment j'ai vendu des sous-marins à partir de ma vieille maison rurale en France

Comment j'ai vendu des sous-marins à partir de ma vieille maison rurale en France

William Skyvington

GAMONE PRESS

Partie 1
Mes articles de blog

http://skyvington.blogspot.fr

mot-clef "submarines"

Australia's submarines

It has just been announced that Australia plans to build "the world's most lethal conventional submarine fleet". That curious expression is an example of the propensity to exaggerate whenever Australians talk about Australia. It's a little like referring, say, to "the world's most powerful horse-cavalry division". If foreign navies throughout the world were to reach a gentlemen's agreement with Australia to the effect that only classic diesel-powered submersible vessels would be employed in future underwater conflicts with the Royal Australian Navy, then we would probably be in a relatively comfortable situation. But, if an uncouth enemy were to ignore the rules of the game by using attack submarines of the nuclear-powered SSN class (not to be confused with submarines that actually launch nuclear missiles), then Australia's antiquated SSG models might not be nearly as "deadly" as claimed.

Australia's recent history in the submarine domain, dating from the Bob Hawke era and culminating in the existence of six faulty Australian-made Collins-class vessels, has been catastrophic, from both a financial and a technological viewpoint. Will the situation be better when these old-fashioned mediocre submarines (whose computer systems are off-the-shelf products from Raytheon) are replaced around 2025 by the newer models, to be manufactured by the same shipbuilder?

As an outside observer knowing little about defense strategies in general and submarines in particular, I have the impression that the decision that has just been announced has been largely inspired by the cogitations of an Australian think tank named Kokoda.

For $22 you can even purchase a paper signed by Ross Babbage, dated April 2007, entitled Australia's Future Underwater Operations and System Requirements. Although I haven't yet invested in a copy of this report (and no doubt never will, because I've got more exciting stuff to read), I'm convinced that the decision of the Royal Australian Navy reflects intimately the thinking of the above-named author. So, it would appear to be a blatant case of one-man thinking. What a tank for submarines! Incidentally, at the Kokoda website, the summary of Babbage's report is accompanied by a quaint drawing:

Don't you agree with me that this rudimentary sketch looks like an illustration from an old volume by Jules Verne? If you look closely, you can even see a midget robot submarine that has emerged from the entrails of the mother vessel. Believe it or not, this is an authentic aspect of Australia's future submarine fleet. Vicious little unmanned tadpoles will be expected to do all the dirty work while the host vessel sits quietly on the seabed, trying to remain undetected.

Recently, I got into a discussion with an Australian friend concerning the antiquated nature of the transport infrastructure in New South Wales. I was thinking primarily of roads, bridges and railway lines. He reacted simplistically by claiming that the volume of tax revenues in Australia is insufficient to cover expenditure in this domain. Now, that sounds to me like naive bullshit. In Australia, the land is composed of metaphorical gold. Theoretically, there are more than enough riches in Australia's soil to build the world's greatest roads, bridges, railway lines and nuclear-powered submarines. There's enough uranium in Australia to power all the nuclear vessels of all the navies of the globe. The only vital natural resource that is totally lacking in Australia is political consciousness. The concept of statesmanship is unknown in Australia. Politicians get elected because they promise, say, to lower interest rates for wage-earners paying mortgages on their suburban houses. Australians voters simply don't comprehend the notion of electing an individual with political wisdom, vision, imagination and profound humanitarian moral principles (as distinct from the candidate's uninteresting personal beliefs of a religious kind). For loud-mouthed snake-oil candidates, seeking to be elected, mythical Australia is the richest land on Earth... and I agree with them a priori. But, for elected representatives of the nation, there's never enough cash in the coffers to build a safe road, a modern bridge, a decent train service or a self-respecting nuclear-powered submarine.

An article in this morning's The Australian says: Although Defence has not yet ruled out the possibility of Australia acquiring nuclear-powered submarines, this option is considered highly unlikely on strategic, practical and political grounds.

Note the final adjective: political. That's what I was saying a moment ago: Australia is simply not mature enough, politically, to own a fleet of nuclear-powered submarines. As the old saying goes, or might have gone: Every nation has the submarines it deserves.

Sous-marins de l'Australie

It has just been announced that Australia plans to build "the world's most lethal conventional submarine fleet". That curious expression is an example of the propensity to exaggerate whenever Australians talk about Australia. It's a little like referring, say, to "the world's most powerful horse-cavalry division". If foreign navies throughout the world were to reach a gentlemen's agreement with Australia to the effect that only classic diesel-powered submersible vessels would be employed in future underwater conflicts with the Royal Australian Navy, then we would probably be in a relatively comfortable situation. But, if an uncouth enemy were to ignore the rules of the game by using attack submarines of the nuclear-powered SSN class (not to be confused with submarines that actually launch nuclear missiles), then Australia's antiquated SSG models might not be nearly as "deadly" as claimed.

On vient d'annoncer que l'Australie compte construire "la flottille de sous-marins conventionnels la plus létale au monde". Cette expression curieuse est un exemple de l'habitude d'exagérer chaque fois que des Australiens parlent au sujet de l'Australie. C'est un peu comme si l'on parlait de "la division de cavalerie la plus puisante au monde". Si les forces navales de toute la planète se mettait d'accord à n'exploiter uniquement que des sous-marins conventionnels dans tout conflit avec l'Australie, nous serions alors dans une position relativement confortable. Mais, si un ennemi malpoli ne respectait pas les règles du jeu, en utilisant des sous-marins d'attaque de la classe SSN (à ne pas confondre avec des sous-marins capables de lancer des missiles nucléaires), alors les vieux modèles SSG de l'Australie pourraient ne pas être aussi "létaux" qu'on le dise.

Australia's recent history in the submarine domain, dating from the Bob Hawke era and culminating in the existence of six faulty Australian-made Collins-class vessels, has been catastrophic, from both a financial and a technological viewpoint. Will the situation be better when these old-fashioned mediocre submarines (whose computer systems are off-the-shelf products from Raytheon) are replaced around 2025 by the newer models, to be manufactured by the same shipbuilder?

L'histoire récente de l'Australie dans le domaine des sous-marins, qui date de l'époque Bob Hawke et qui a abouti à six engins *made-in-Australia* de la classe Collins, a été catastrophique, d'un point de vue à la fois financier et technologique. La situation sera-t-elle meilleure quand ces sous-marins vieillots (dont les systèmes informatiques sont des produits Raythéon de boutique) auront été remplacés par de nouveaux modèles du même chantier naval ?

As an outside observer knowing little about defense strategies in general and submarines in particular, I have the impression that the decision that has just been announced has been largely inspired by the cogitations of an Australian think tank named Kokoda.

En tant qu'observateur d'extérieur ne connaissant presque rien sur les stratégies de défense en général et sur les sous-marins en particulier, j'ai l'impression que la décision qui vient d'être annoncée s'est inspirée largement des cogitations d'un think-tank australien nommé Kokoda.

For $22 you can even purchase a paper signed by Ross Babbage, dated April 2007, entitled Australia's Future Underwater Operations and System Requirements. Although I haven't yet invested in a copy of this report (and no doubt never will, because I've got more exciting stuff to read), I'm convinced that the decision of the Royal Australian Navy reflects intimately the thinking of the above-named author. So, it would appear to be a blatant case of one-man thinking. What a tank for submarines! Incidentally, at the Kokoda website, the summary of Babbage's report is accompanied by a quaint drawing:

Pour la somme de $22 vous pouvez même acheter un papier signé de Ross Babbage, daté d'avril 2007, intitulé *Australia's Future Underwater Operations and System Requirements*. Bien que je ne me sois encore pas payé un exemplaire de ce rapport (chose que je ne ferai sans doute jamais, car j'ai des écrits plus passionnants à lire), je suis convaincu que la décision de la Marine royale australienne réflète directement les pensées de l'auteur quie je viens de mentionner. Il s'agirait donc d'un cas criant de pensée à homme unique. Quel drôle de *think-tank* pour un sous-marin ! Sur le site Kokoda, les conclusions du rapport de Babbage s'accompagnent d'un dessin vieux-style :

Don't you agree with me that this rudimentary sketch looks like an illustration from an old volume by Jules Verne? If you look closely, you can even see a midget robot submarine that has emerged from the entrails of the mother vessel. Believe it or not, this is an authentic aspect of Australia's future submarine fleet. Vicious little unmanned tadpoles will be expected to do all the dirty work while the host vessel sits quietly on the seabed, trying to remain undetected.

Ne pensez-vous pas, comme moi, que ce croquis rudimentaire ressemble à une illustration issue d'un vieux tome de Jules Verne ? Si vous le regardez de près, vous verrez même qu'un minuscule sous-marin robotique quitte le ventre du vaisseau maternel. Croyez-le-moi, il s'agit d'un aspect authentique de la flotte future australienne de sous-marins. On a le sentiment que de méchants petite têtards feront tout le sale boulot pendant que le vaisseau principal reste silencieusement sur le fond, essayant de ne pas être détecté.

Recently, I got into a discussion with an Australian friend concerning the antiquated nature of the transport infrastructure in New South Wales. I was thinking primarily of roads, bridges and railway lines. He reacted simplistically by claiming that the volume of tax revenues in Australia is insufficient to cover expenditure in this domain. Now, that sounds to me like naive bullshit. In Australia, the land is composed of metaphorical gold. Theoretically, there are more than enough riches in Australia's soil to build the world's greatest roads, bridges, railway lines and nuclear-powered submarines. There's enough uranium in Australia to power all the nuclear vessels of all the navies of the globe. The only vital natural resource that is totally lacking in Australia is political consciousness. The concept of statesmanship is unknown in Australia. Politicians get elected because they promise, say, to lower interest rates for wage-earners paying mortgages on their suburban houses. Australians voters simply don't comprehend the notion of electing an individual with political wisdom, vision, imagination and profound humanitarian moral principles (as distinct from the candidate's uninteresting personal beliefs of a religious kind). For loud-mouthed snake-oil candidates, seeking to be elected, mythical Australia is the richest land on Earth... and I agree with them a priori. But, for elected representatives of the nation, there's never enough cash in the coffers to build a safe road, a modern bridge, a decent train service or a self-respecting nuclear-powered submarine.

J'ai eu récemment une discussion avec un ami australien concernant la nature antique de l'infrastructure des transports en commun en New South Wales. Je pensais surtout aux routes, aux ponts, aux lignes de chemin du fer. Cet ami réagit de façon primaire en disant que le volume des revenus fiscaux en Australie n'était pas suffisant pour couvrir les investissements nécessaires dans ce domaine. A mes yeux, c'était une réaction stupide. En Australie, la terre entière est métaphoriquement dorée. Théoriquement, il ya des richesses plus que suffisantes en Australie pour construire des routes, des ponts et des chemins de fer qui seraient les plus beaux de toute la planète... ainsi que des sous-marins à propulsion nucléaire. Il y a assez d'uranium en Australie pour propulser tous les navires nucléaires de toutes les marines nationales de la planète Terre. La seule ressource qui manque totalement en Australie est un discernement politique. Le concept d'homme d'état est peu connu en Australie. Un homme politique se fait élire parce qu'il promet, disons, de baisser les taux d'intérêt chez les travailleurs qui achètent leurs bicoques de banlieue. Les électeurs australiens ne comprenent pas l'idée de choisir un candidat qui possède de la sagesse politique, de la vision, de l'imagination et des principes humains profonds sur le plan moral (rien à voir avec ses convictions d'ordre religieux). Un candidat marchand de remèdes de charlatan trouve effectivement que l'Australie est un pays très riche... pour lui ! Mais d'autres élus de la nation osent croire qu'il n'y a pas assez de sous pour construire une bonne route, un pont moderne, un bon service de chemin de fer... ou alors un sous-marin à propulsion nucléaire.

An article in this morning's The Australian says: Although Defence has not yet ruled out the possibility of Australia acquiring nuclear-powered submarines, this option is considered highly unlikely on strategic, practical and political grounds.

Un article dans *The Australian* de ce matin dit : Bien que la Défense n'exclut pas la possibilité que l'Australie achète des sous-marins de propulsion nucléaire, cette option est hautement improbable pour des raisons stratégiques, pratiques et politiques.

Note the final adjective: political. That's what I was saying a moment ago: Australia is simply not mature enough, politically, to own a fleet of nuclear-powered submarines. As the old saying goes, or might have gone: Every nation has the submarines it deserves.

Remarquez ce dernier adjectif : politique. C'est ce que je disais tout à l'heure : l'Australie n'est simplement pas assez mûre, politiquement, pour être propriétaire d'une flotte de sous-marins à propulsion nucléaire. Comme dit le vieux dicton (ou aurait pu dire) : Chaque nation possède les sous-marins qu'elle mérite.

Australian arithmetic

During my short trip to Australia in 2006, I was shocked to discover that there were no trains to a couple of NSW towns that I wished to visit (Braidwood and Byron Bay), and I was further surprised to find that the only way of crossing the river at Grafton was by means of the antiquated bridge over which I used to pedal my bicycle when I was a boy.

Since then, I've got into the habit of asking naive questions about Australia's infrastructures. Why do Australians never stop boasting about the fabulous wealth of their land, while still tolerating old-fashioned infrastructures that are often like those of a developing nation? A friend tried to tell me recently that the respective infrastructures of France and Australia cannot be compared because... there are three times as many tax-payers in France as in Australia. This analysis is rubbish, of course. When Australia sells a mountain of precious minerals to foreign purchasers, her potential income from the deal has nothing whatsoever to do with the number of Aussies paying taxes. It's a matter of complex political, economic and business considerations that determine what percentage of such wealth will return to Australian citizens, and how much will be left in the hands of greedy international capitalists. It's childishly naive to imagine that the quality of Australia's roads, bridges and railway lines depends necessarily and exclusively upon the financial resources resulting from income tax paid by Aussie wage-earners. That is not only bad arithmetic; it's bad politics. And you can't run a country on such idiotic principles. If indeed the mountains of minerals that we're peddling to foreign buyers don't enable the citizens of Australia to take advantage of decent infrastructures, then our nation's leaders should halt immediately the sale of these mountains of minerals, while we do some serious thinking about what has gone wrong.

Let me turn my attention to another kind of infrastructure. In my articles entitled Australia's submarines [display] and Nuclear energy [display], I referred to an aspect of Australia's future defense system that has given rise to articles in the local press over the last few days. All these articles repeat the same huge investment figure: some 25 billion dollars for six future submarines. Now, this is typically the kind of situation in which a citizen, instead of believing naively what he hears, has the right and the possibility to do some independent thinking. Let's talk in euros. The unit cost of each of Australia's future submarines amounts to 2.75 billion euros. And what is Australia going to receive for this sum? An old-fashioned vessel that runs on diesel oil. My God, that's a lot of cash for a diesel boat!

By way of comparison, let us look at the production of one of the world's most advanced nations in the field of nuclear-propelled submarines: France. It just so happens that France, like Australia, is currently planning to renew its fleet of six attack submarines. The future model is known as the Barracuda, and it will be constructed in the Cherbourg shipyards in Normandy.

The Barracuda vessels will, of course, be propelled by nuclear energy. So, they will be intrinsically far more sophisticated than Australia's classic vessels. And the Barracuda's unit cost price? One billion euros. In other words, Australia's classic submarine, to be delivered in 2025, will be 2.75 times as expensive as France's avant-garde nuclear vessel, to be delivered eight years earlier, in 2017.

Is there something wrong with my arithmetic? Or is there maybe something wrong with Australia's political thinking about the nation's allegedly high-priced infrastructures?

Arithmétique australienne

During my short trip to Australia in 2006, I was shocked to discover that there were no trains to a couple of NSW towns that I wished to visit (Braidwood and Byron Bay), and I was further surprised to find that the only way of crossing the river at Grafton was by means of the antiquated bridge over which I used to pedal my bicycle when I was a boy.

Au cours d'un bref voyage en Australie en 2006, j'étais choqué de découvrir qu'il n'y avait pas de liaisons ferroviaires avec deux villes que j'aurais aimé visiter (Braidwood et Byron Bay), et j'étais surpris davantage quand j'ai découvert que la seule manière de traverser le fleuve à Grafton était par le pont archaïque sur lequel je passais en bicyclette quand j'étais un gamin.

Since then, I've got into the habit of asking naive questions about Australia's infrastructures. Why do Australians never stop boasting about the fabulous wealth of their land, while still tolerating old-fashioned infrastructures that are often like those of a developing nation? A friend tried to tell me recently that the respective infrastructures of France and Australia cannot be compared because... there are three times as many tax-payers in France as in Australia. This analysis is rubbish, of course. When Australia sells a mountain of precious minerals to foreign purchasers, her potential income from the deal has nothing whatsoever to do with the number of Aussies paying taxes. It's a matter of complex political, economic and business considerations that determine what percentage of such wealth will return to Australian citizens, and how much will be left in the hands of greedy international capitalists. It's childishly naive to imagine that the quality of Australia's roads, bridges and railway lines depends necessarily and exclusively upon the financial resources resulting from income tax paid by Aussie wage-earners. That is not only bad arithmetic; it's bad politics. And you can't run a country on such idiotic principles. If indeed the mountains of minerals that we're peddling to foreign buyers don't enable the citizens of Australia to take advantage of decent infrastructures, then our nation's leaders should halt immediately the sale of these mountains of minerals, while we do some serious thinking about what has gone wrong.

Depuis cette époque, je me suis mis à poser certaines questions naïves sur les infrastructures de l'Australie. Pourquoi les Australiens ne cessent-tils jamais de se vanter des richesses fabuleuses de leur pays, tout en se contentant d'infrastructures archaïques dignes d'un pays sous-développé ? Un ancien camarade m'a dit récemment que l'on ne devrait pas comparer les infrastructures respectives de la France et l'Australie car... il y a trois fois plus de contribuables en France qu'en Australie. Cette analyse est ridicule, bien entendu. Quand l'Australie vend une montagne de minerai à un client étranger, ses revenus potentiels créés par cette vente n'ont rien à voir avec le nombre de travailleurs australiens qui paient des impôts. Il s'agit de considérations complexes d'ordre politique, économique et commercial qui déterminent quel est le pourcentage de ces revenus qui sera rendu aux citoyens australiens, et combien restera dans les poches de capitalistes internationaux voraces. Il est puéril d'imaginer un seul instant que la qualité des routes, des ponts et des lignes de chemin de fer puisse dépendre forcément et exclusivement des versements au fisc effectués par de petits contribuables australiens. Il ne s'agit pas de la mauvaise arithmétique; mais d'une mauvaise compréhension de la politique d'une nation. Et l'on ne dirige pas une nation selon de tels principes idiots. S'il est vrai que les montagnes de minerai que l'on vend aux acheteurs étrangers ne permettent pas aux citoyens d'Australie de bénéficier d'infrastructures décentes, alors nos leaders de la nation devraient faire cesser immédiatement la mise en vente de ces montagnes pendant que nous pensons sérieusement à ce qui a foiré.

Let me turn my attention to another kind of infrastructure. In my articles entitled Australia's submarines [display] and Nuclear energy [display], I referred to an aspect of Australia's future defense system that has given rise to articles in the local press over the last few days. All these articles repeat the same huge investment figure: some 25 billion dollars for six future submarines. Now, this is typically the kind of situation in which a citizen, instead of believing naively what he hears, has the right and the possibility to do some independent thinking. Let's talk in euros. The unit cost of each of Australia's future submarines amounts to 2.75 billion euros. And what is Australia going to receive for this sum? An old-fashioned vessel that runs on diesel oil. My God, that's a lot of cash for a diesel boat!

Permettez-moi de regarder un autre type d'infrastructure. Dans mes articles intitulés **Australia's submarines** [display] et **Nuclear energy** [display], j'ai fait allusion à un aspect du futur système de défence qui a donné lieu aux articles de presse depuis quelques jours. Touys ces articles citent le même chiffre d'investissement gigantesque : quelques 25 milliards de dollars pour six sous-marins futurs. Or, c'est une situation typique où un citoyen, au lieu de croire naïvement ce qu'il entend, a le droit et la possibilité de réfléchir de façon indépendante. Parlons en euros. Le coût unitaire de chacun des sous-marins futurs de l'Australie correspond à 2,75 milliards d'euros [*erreur WS*]. Et que va recevoir l'Australie pour cette somme-là ? Un vaisseau vieux style qui marche au diesel. Mon Dieu, ça fait cher pour acheter un bateau diesel !

By way of comparison, let us look at the production of one of the world's most advanced nations in the field of nuclear-propelled submarines: France. It just so happens that France, like Australia, is currently planning to renew its fleet of six attack submarines. The future model is known as the Barracuda, and it will be constructed in the Cherbourg shipyards in Normandy.

A titre de comparaison, regardons la production de l'une des nations les plus avancées du monde dans le domaine des sous-marins à propulsion nucléaire : la France. Le hasard fait que la France, comme l'Australie, compte remplacer actuellement sa flotte de six sous-marins d'attaque. Leur modèle du futur s'appelle le Barracuda, et il sera fabriqué à Cherbourg en Normandie.

The Barracuda vessels will, of course, be propelled by nuclear energy. So, they will be intrinsically far more sophisticated than Australia's classic vessels. And the Barracuda's unit cost price?

One billion euros. In other words, Australia's classic submarine, to be delivered in 2025, will be 2.75 times as expensive as France's avant-garde nuclear vessel, to be delivered eight years earlier, in 2017.

Ces vaisseaux Barracuda seront propulsés, bien entendu, par de l'énergie nucléaire. C'est-à-dire qu'ils seront intrinsèquement beaucoup plus sophistiqués que les vaisseaux classiques de l'Australie. Et le prix unitaire du Barracuda ? Un milliard d'euros [*erreur WS*]. En d'autres termes, le sous-marin classique de l'Australie, livré en 2025, sera 2,75 fois plus cher que le sous-marin d'avant-garde nucléaire de la France, livré huit ans auparavant, en 2017.

Is there something wrong with my arithmetic? Or is there maybe something wrong with Australia's political thinking about the nation's allegedly high-priced infrastructures?

Y a-t-il une erreur dans mon arithmétique ? Ou y a-t-il quelque chose qui cloche dans les pensées politiques de l'Australie concernant ses projets d'infrastructure trop coûteux ?

Expensive, aesthetic and nasty

An inspired TV journalist once asked the Dalai Lama: "Can your beliefs in reincarnation and your unbounded respect for all forms of life be reconciled with the case, say, of a mosquito that's intent upon settling on your arm and sucking your blood?" The grinning Dalai Lama said he would try to shoo the creature away. The journalist insisted: "But what if the mosquito fails to go away, because it's determined to bite you?" The Dalai Lama broke into typical laughter and made it clear by a few unmistakable gestures that, in such circumstances, the creature stood a good chance of being squashed to death. I admired the Dalai Lama's suggestion that it's all very well to have lofty principles... but, if an alien creature is attacking you, then it's perfectly normal to exterminate the vicious little bugger. [On the other hand, maybe I totally misunderstood what the wise man was saying.]

I can't say I've ever felt the need to respect religiously all forms of life, because I grew up in an environment where it was quite normal to kill various animals: snakes, rabbits, hens, ducks, etc. It's true, though, that I was overcome by pangs of guilt for several days, at around the age of ten, after having shot an unsuspecting bird with a catapult. [Even today, I remain so marked by that anecdote that I recently wove it into my fictional biography of Master Bruno, the medieval hermit who founded the Carthusian order of Christian monks.] I'm not cynical to the point of saying that rules are made to be broken, but I believe that we have the right—and the obligation, at times—to stretch them to their breaking point... and what the hell if they snap! That's why I like the Dalai Lama's loose attitude towards offensive mosquitoes, as opposed, say, to the dogmatic outlook of many Christian prelates concerning aborted foetuses or human stem cells.

In a neighboring moral domain, I've never been an all-out pacifist, either. For example, I've always been horrified by the alleged "turning the other cheek" principle of Christianity [which, I believe, has rarely been put into regular practice]. If I had been a

Christian in one of Rome's martyrdom arenas, I would have used every possible means at my disposal in order to kill the beasts before they killed me.

And that brings me to the subject of the present post: modern machines of destruction. I was happy to see that some privileged Australian military personnel have been undergoing training in France in the context of the purchase by my native land of several Franco-German combat helicopters of the Tiger class. Now, if you haven't seen these diabolical but fascinating beasts in action, you might take a look at the following spectacular video:

Jumping from helicopters to submarines [metaphorically], I feel obliged to add a few remarks concerning the subject I tackled briefly in my article of 2 January 2008 entitled Australian arithmetic [display]. Otherwise, I could be accused of expressing opinions and then leaving them hanging up in the air, without following them right on through. Let me repeat rapidly the essential points of my reflections concerning the high price of Australia's future submarines. The Australian press had announced that our country would be spending 25 billion dollars to build six diesel-powered vessels, and I made the remark that French nuclear-powered combat submarines of the Barracuda class can be purchased for 36% of that outlay: a billion euros per submarine.

At the same time that I made those remarks publicly in my blog, I got into direct contact with Ross Babbage, chairman of the Kokoda Foundation in Canberra. He's the man who actually signed the Kokoda paper #4 of April 2007, which was the main source of the media articles that had presented this submarine affair to the public, as explained in my article of 26 December 2007 entitled Australia's submarines [display]. Ross Babbage reacted kindly by sending me (airmail to France) a complimentary copy of his report, along with helpful explanations that clarify the situation considerably. Here are the precise words on this subject from the Kokoda paper #4:

... simply replacing the Collins Class submarines with a new class of six submarines would probably cost $12-$15 billion.

Modernising and adapting Australia's total underwater capabilities to meet the needs of potential defence contingencies in the 2025-2050 timeframe would probably require expenditures in the order of $20-$25 billion.

In other words, we are down to a unit price of $2-$2.5 billion per vessel. Expressed in European currency, that's a unit price between 1.2 and 1.5 billion euros. It's still 20% to 50% more expensive than the ultramodern French nuclear-powered Barracuda submarine, but we're down to sensible figures. Incidentally, the expression "Australia's total underwater capabilities" includes, besides the six future submarines, such costly matters as RAN anti-submarine warfare capabilities and RAAF underwater-surveillance capabilities.

Now, the Antipodes blog is hardly the right place to get deeply involved in affairs of this kind. All I wish to say, by way of a conclusion, is that I was rather surprised by the relatively "lightweight" nature of the Kokoda paper, which is a tiny printed booklet of no more than 64 pages. I had been expecting that the so-called "paper" would be a dense fact-filled report stored, maybe, on a set of DVDs. On the contrary, it skims through the domain of submarines with no attempt whatsoever at attaining depth. Astonishing in the case of a report on submarines...

Chers, beaux et méchants

An inspired TV journalist once asked the Dalai Lama: "Can your beliefs in reincarnation and your unbounded respect for all forms of life be reconciled with the case, say, of a mosquito that's intent upon settling on your arm and sucking your blood?" The grinning Dalai Lama said he would try to shoo the creature away. The journalist insisted: "But what if the mosquito fails to go away, because it's determined to bite you?" The Dalai Lama broke into typical laughter and made it clear by a few unmistakable gestures that, in such circumstances, the creature stood a good chance of being squashed to death. I admired the Dalai Lama's suggestion that it's all very well to have lofty principles... but, if an alien creature is attacking you, then it's perfectly normal to exterminate the vicious little bugger. [On the other hand, maybe I totally misunderstood what the wise man was saying.]

Un journaliste télé bien inspiré demanda une fois au Dalaï Lama : *"Vos croyances sur le plan de la réincarnation et votre respect sans limites de toute forme de vie peuvent-ils se reconcilier avec le cas, disons, d'une moustique qui se pose sur votre bras afin de sucer votre sang ?"* Le Dalaï Lama répondit qu'il tenterait alors de chasser la moustique. Le journalist insista : *"Que faire néanmoins si la moustique refuse de partir, parce que son intention unique est de vous piquer ?"* Le Dalaï Lama éclata d'un rire typique et indiqua d'un geste de façon indiscutable que la moustique serait alors vite écrasé. J'ai beaucoup aimé l'attitude du Dalaï Lama. On a beau avoir de principes élévés... mais, en fin de compte, lorsqu'une créature étrangère s'attaque à vous, il est parfaitement normal de tenter de détruire le petit ennemi. [Il se peut que j'interprète mal les mots et les gestes du sage homme.]

I can't say I've ever felt the need to respect religiously all forms of life, because I grew up in an environment where it was quite normal to kill various animals: snakes, rabbits, hens, ducks, etc. It's true, though, that I was overcome by pangs of guilt for several days, at around the age of ten, after having shot an unsuspecting bird with a catapult. [Even today, I remain so marked by that anecdote that I recently wove it into my fictional biography of Master Bruno, the medieval hermit who founded the Carthusian order of Christian monks.] I'm not cynical to the point of saying that rules are made to be broken, but I believe that we have the right—and the obligation, at times—to stretch them to their breaking point... and what the hell if they snap! That's why I like the Dalai Lama's loose attitude towards offensive mosquitoes, as opposed, say, to the dogmatic outlook of many Christian prelates concerning aborted foetuses or human stem cells.

Je ne pourrais pas affirmer ressentir le besoin de respecter religieusement toutes les formes de vie, parce que j'ai grandi dans une ambiance où il était tout à fait normal de tuer certains animaux : serpents, lapins, poules, canards, etc. Il est tout de même vrai que j'étais troublé pendant plusieurs jours par des sentiments de honte après avoir tué par inadvertance au moyen d'une lance-pierre un oiseau de passage. [Même aujourd'hui, je suis resté tellement marqué par cet événement que j'ai inséré cette anecdote dans une biographie fictive sur Bruno, l'ermite chrétien du Moyen Age qui fonda l'ordre cartusien.] Je ne suis pas cynique au point de dire que toutes les règles sont prêtes à être violées, mais je considère néanmoins que nous avons le droit, sinon parfois l'obligation, de les étendre aux limites... et peu importe si elles se cassent. Voilà pourquoi j'ai aimé l'attitude du Dalaï Lama envers les moustiques qui nous attaquent... tellement différentes des principes dogmatiques des prélats chrétiens sur l'avortement et l'exploitation de cellules souche.

In a neighboring moral domain, I've never been an all-out pacifist, either. For example, I've always been horrified by the alleged "turning the other cheek" principle of Christianity [which, I believe, has rarely been put into regular practice]. If I had been a Christian in one of Rome's martyrdom arenas, I would have used every possible means at my disposal in order to kill the beasts before they killed me.

Sur un autre plan moral, je nai jamais été un pacifiste pur et dur. Par exemple, je ne partage pas le principe chrétien qui consiste à tendre l'autre joue (peu exploité, à mes yeux, sur le plan pratique).

Si j'avais été un chrétien à Rome, j'aurais tout fait pour détruire les fauves avant qu'elles se dirigent vers moi.

And that brings me to the subject of the present post: modern machines of destruction. I was happy to see that some privileged Australian military personnel have been undergoing training in France in the context of the purchase by my native land of several Franco-German combat helicopters of the Tiger class. Now, if you haven't seen these diabolical but fascinating beasts in action, you might take a look at the following spectacular video:

Et ça m'amène su sujet de cet article : des appareils modernes de destruction. J'étais content de voir que du personnel militaire australien qui s'entraînait en France dans le contexte de l'achat par l'Australie de plusieurs hélicoptères de la catégorie Tigre. Si vous navez jamais vu ces monstres en action, je vous propose de regarder la vidéo suivante :

Jumping from helicopters to submarines [metaphorically], I feel obliged to add a few remarks concerning the subject I tackled briefly in my article of 2 January 2008 entitled Australian arithmetic [display]. Otherwise, I could be accused of expressing opinions and then leaving them hanging up in the air, without following them right on through. Let me repeat rapidly the essential points of my reflections concerning the high price of Australia's future submarines. The Australian press had announced that our country would be spending 25 billion dollars to build six diesel-powered vessels, and I made the remark that French nuclear-powered combat submarines of the Barracuda class can be purchased for 36% of that outlay: a billion d'euros per submarine.

Je saute (métaphoriquement) des hélicoptères aux sous-marins. Je souhaite faiore quelques remarques au sujet abordé dans mon article du 2 janvier 2008 : ***Arithmétique australienne***. Sinon, on pourrait dire que je lance des opinions sans les développer. Je répète donc rapidement ma conviction concernant le prix élevé des sous-marins que l'Australie compte acquérir. La presse australienne a dit que notre pays dépenserait 25 milliards de dollars pour la construction de six vaisseaux à propulsion diesel, ce qui m'a poussé à dire que des sous-marins français à propulsion nucléaire, de la catégorie Barracuda, pourraient s'acheter pour 36% de ces dépenses : un milliard d'euros par sous-marin [*erreur WS*].

At the same time that I made those remarks publicly in my blog, I got into direct contact with Ross Babbage, chairman of the Kokoda Foundation in Canberra. He's the man who actually signed the Kokoda paper #4 of April 2007, which was the main source of the media articles that had presented this submarine affair to the public, as explained in my article of 26 December 2007 entitled Australia's submarines [display]. Ross Babbage reacted kindly by sending me (airmail to France) a complimentary copy of his report, along with helpful explanations that clarify the situation considerably. Here are the precise words on this subject from the Kokoda paper #4:

Au même moment où j'ai fait pûbliquement ces remarques dans mon blog, j'ai pris contact directement avec Ross Babbage, chef de la Fondation Kokoda à Canberra.

... simply replacing the Collins Class submarines with a new class of six submarines would probably cost $12-$15 billion. Modernising and adapting Australia's total underwater capabilities to meet the needs of potential defence contingencies in the 2025-2050 timeframe would probably require expenditures in the order of $20-$25 billion.

… rien que le remplacement des vaisseaux Collins par une nouvelle classe de six sous-marins coûterait probablement de 12 à 15 milliards de dollars. La modernisation et l'adaptation de l'ensemble des capacités totales de l'Australie, pôur répondre aux besoins de la défense de 2025 à 2050 nécessiterait sans doute des dépenses de l'ordre de 20 à 25 milliards de dollars.

In other words, we are down to a unit price of $2-$2.5 billion per vessel. Expressed in European currency, that's a unit price between 1.2 and 1.5 billion euros. It's still 20% to 50% more expensive than the ultramodern French nuclear-powered Barracuda submarine, but we're down to sensible figures. Incidentally, the

Autrement dit, nous arrivons au prix unitaire de 2 à 2,5 milliards de dollars. En monnaie européenne, ça représente un prix unitaire entre 1,2 et 1,5 milliards d'euros. Ça fait néanmoins 20% à 50% plus cher que le sous-marin français Barracuda ultra-moderne à propulsion nucléaire, mais nous sommes arrivés enfin à des chiffres compréhensibles. Soit dit en passant que l'expression australienne "capacités sous-marines totales" couvre, en dehors des six vaisseaux futurs, certaines opérations coûteuses : actions militaires RAN à proprement parler de type anti-sous-marins ennemis, et capacités de surveillance RAAF sous l'eau.

Le blog Antipodes n'est guère une bonne plate-forme pour s'immiscer dans des affaires de ce type. Tout ce que je compte dire, à titre de conclusion, c'est que j'étais plutôt étonné par les dimensions "légères" du document Kokoda : une petite brochure d'à peine 64 pages. Je m'attendais à ce que ce soi-disant "papier" serait un rapport dense stocké normalement sur un ensemble de DVDs. Au contraire, il traverse le domaine des sous-marins sans aucune tentative de descendre dans les profondeurs. Etonnant dans le cas d'un rapport sur les sous-marins…

Did Australia take notice of my advice of 2008 about the superior qualities of French submarines?

In my blog post of January 21, 2008 entitled Expensive, aesthetic and nasty [click here], I made an out-of-the-way suggestion: If Australia's armed forces wish to purchase a new fleet of excellent submarines, why don't they examine what France has to offer? At the same time that I made those remarks publicly in my blog, I got into direct contact with Ross Babbage, chairman of the Kokoda Foundation in Canberra. He's the man who actually signed the Kokoda paper #4 of April 2007, which was the main source of the media articles that had presented this submarine affair to the public, as explained in my article of 26 December 2007 entitled Australia's submarines [click here]. Ross Babbage reacted kindly by sending me (airmail to France) a complimentary copy of his report, along with helpful explanations that clarified the situation considerably.

For the moment, I don't know whether Australia has reached a decision on this question. But I heard yesterday that France is highly placed.

L'Australie a-t-elle tenu compte de mes conseils sur les qualités supérieures de sous-marins français ?

In my blog post of January 21, 2008 entitled Expensive, aesthetic and nasty [click here], I made an out-of-the-way suggestion: If Australia's armed forces wish to purchase a new fleet of excellent submarines, why don't they examine what France has to offer? At the same time that I made those remarks publicly in my blog, I got into direct contact with Ross Babbage, chairman of the Kokoda Foundation in Canberra. He's the man who actually signed the Kokoda paper #4 of April 2007, which was the main source of the media articles that had presented this submarine affair to the public, as explained in my article of 26 December 2007 entitled Australia's submarines [click here]. Ross Babbage reacted kindly by sending me (airmail to France) a complimentary copy of his report, along with helpful explanations that clarified the situation considerably.

Dans mon article du 21 janvier 2008 intitulé *Chers, beaux et méchants*, j'ai fait une suggestion peu banale : Si les forces armées de l'Australie comptent acheter une nouvelle flotte d'excellents sous-marins, pourquoi n'examineraient-elles pas ce qu'offre la France ? Au même moment où j'ai lancé publiquement ces remarques dans mon blog, j'ai pris contact avec Ross Babbage, chef de la Fondation Kokoda à Canberra. Il s'agit de l'individu qui a signé le papier Kokoda n° 4 d'avril 2007, la source principale des articles des média qui avaient présenté cette affaire au public comme je l'ai dit dans mon article du 26 décembre 2007 intitulé Sous-marins de l'Australie. Ross Babbage réagit cordialement par l'envoi (courrier postal vers la France) d'un exemplaire gratuit de son rapport, accompagné d'explications utiles qui ont clarifié considérablement la situation.

For the moment, I don't know whether Australia has reached a decision on this question. But I heard yesterday that France is highly placed.

Pour le moment, je ne sais pas si l'Australie a pris une décision sur cette question. Mais j'ai entendu dire hier que la France est haut placée.

Partie 2
Mes tentatives de contacts avec la présidence

Validation n° 1 — le 11 juillet 2017

Je suis l'individu qui a parlé à l'Australie dès 2007 de l'intérêt d'examiner les sous-marins de fabrication DCNS. Cette information a donné lieu à un marché gigantesque de l'ordre de 50 milliards de dollars australiens.

Il est temps que mon rôle dans cette affaire soit reconnu.

J'ai besoin d'une adresse email pour que le président puisse lire mon article soumis il y a une semaine au New York Times. Cet article contient 5 liens vers mon blog Antipodes.

PS Pour le président Macron : Je suis un ancien prof d'anglais au lycée Henri IV.

Validation n° 2 — le 11 juillet 2017

Monsieur le Président : Je suis scandalisé par l'incapacité de l'ambassade à Canberra à transmettre mon article qui révèle que j'étais l'individu franco-australien qui a signalé à l'Australie, en 2007, les avantages de sous-marins DCNS.

Voir mon blog Antipodes http://skyvington.blogspot.fr/ et donner le mot-clef "submarines".

Visiblement, l'ambassade à Canberra est fautive, car elle n'a pas fait remonter à l'Elysée mon courriel d'hier. Incompétence inimaginable !

Je suis scandalisé. Du coup, vous n'allez pas m'inviter au défilé du 14 juillet. Tant pis. Je n'aurais pas aimé me retrouver à côté d'un certain invité...

Validation n° 3 — le 11 juillet 2017

Monsieur le président : Au moment où je vois une déclaration commune entre vous et Malcolm Turnbull, ma participation dans cette célébration est sucrée tout simplement parce que des employés de l'ambassade à Canberra sont visiblement incapables de lire le courriel que je leur ai envoyé hier. Où va la France ? Je suis terriblement attristé car je voulais assister en tant que Franco-Australien au défilé du 14 juillet... Toute ma valise était préparée, et je me suis dit que j'allais faire un effort pour rester correct à côté de Trump. Mais tous mes plans sont détruits à cause d'individus à l'ambassade de Canberra qui ne peuvent pas transmettre un simple courriel. Vous comprendrez, Monsieur le Président, que la déception pour moi est infinie. Cordialement, William Skyvington

Validation n° 4 — le 11 juillet 2017

Monsieur le Président : Je disais du mal des services de l'ambassade à Canberra. Peut-être s'agissait-il tout simplement de délais du côté de l'Elysée. Dans ce cas-là, je retire toutes mes observations désobligeantes au sujet de l'ambassade de Canberra. Les communications avec la présidence ne sont pas simples, même pour un vendeur de sous-marins.

Cordialement,

William Skyvington

PS Les communications avec l'Australie sont beaucoup plus difficiles.

Validation n° 5 — le 12 juillet 2017

Monsieur le President,

Vous n'avez jamais entendu parler de moi. Je suis pourtant l'Australien (naturalisé à Grenoble depuis 2009) qui a réussi, à partir de janvier 2008, à convaincre l'Australie d'examiner les sous-marins fabriqués par les chantiers DCNS. Vous connaissez la suite.

Vous trouverez ci-joint un petit résumé publié par le New York Times en juillet 2017. J'espère que vous aurez le temps d'examiner ces informations.

Cordialement,

William Skyvington

How I sold submarines from my farmhouse on the edge of the French Alps

In the lucrative business of selling submarines, I would imagine that most specialists go to extraordinary lengths to study their products and present them to prospective clients throughout the world. I did nothing more than sit in front of my Macintosh and use my Antipodes blog as a sales tool. And my efforts were most successful : some billions of dollars!

The entire story of this colossal sales success can be found in five blog posts.

My first post, dated 26 December 2007, is located at http:// skyvington.blogspot.fr/2007/12/australias-submarines.html. From the outset, my tone was sarcastic, because I found that a certain Ross Babbage talked about submarines as if he were telling a tale by Jules Verne. I even dared to say that my native land was adopting a naive attitude towards defence, as if it were far too expensive for a nation that happened to own some of the planet's greatest deposits of mineral wealth. And I concluded that Australia was politically immature.

In my second post, dated 27 December 2007, located at http:// skyvington.blogspot.fr/2007/12/nuclear-energy.html, I alluded briefly to the unlikely possibility that Australia might look into the idea of nuclear-powered submarines.

My third post, dated 2 January 2008, located at http://skyvington.blogspot.fr/2008/01/australian-arithmetic.html, remained critical of Australia's apparent financial calculations. For the first time, I suggested explicitly that my native land might look into French achievements in this domain.

My fourth post, dated 21 January 2008, located at http://skyvington.blogspot.fr/2008/01/expensive-aesthetic-and-nasty.html, started with an amusing anecdote about the Dalai Lama. Then I returned to the question of financial costs. In a nutshell, Australia seemed to be thinking of spending much money to purchase too little. By that time, my knowledge of the situation was enhanced by my reading of a Kokoda paper sent to me by Ross Babbage. To my naive eyes, it still did not make sense.

Much later, my fifth post, dated 22 April 2016, located at http://skyvington.blogspot.fr/2016/04/did-australia-take-notice-of-my-advice.html, was a reaction to rumors that Australia might indeed have taken notice of my advice as a naive submarine salesman. On 26 April 2016, Australia's prime minister Malcolm Turnbull announced that they had signed a contract with the French DCNS giant to build 12 submarines for AUD 50 billion.

My blog story ends there… but the submarine story itself is only starting down in Australia. Curiously, in spite of my efforts to gain recognition as an amateur submarine salesman, nobody has ever bothered to listen to me. I even have the impression that professional people in this field simply never use the Internet. Are they too far down in the depths of murky waters?

Validation n° 6 — le 12 juillet 2017

Si mes calculs sont justes, vous êtes de retour du G7 et vous risquez de me téléphoner demain matin. Quant à moi, je suis tout à fait prêt à monter à Paris pour le défilé du 14 juillet. Et je promets être sage comme un enfant auprès de votre invité. (Il y a pire que lui à la mairie de Choranche.) Attention : Ma maison est difficile à dénicher. Gamone se trouve juste à côté de Pont-en-Royans. Ne pas utiliser de gadget. On fait un petit km après Pont-en-Royans en direction du Vercors, puis on tourne à gauche (c'est marqué Gamone) en direction de Presles. A peine 100 mètres plus loin, au premier virage (dangereux), un panneau à gauche est marqué Gamone. Mon chien Fitzroy attendra la voiture. A demain. William

Validation n° 7 — le 13 juillet 2017

Je suis déjà parfaitement éveillé. Je dors peu. Je suis en parfaite santé. Et j'attends votre coup de téléphone à 04 76 64 18 32. Vous me trouverez un individu calme et facile, de 76 ans, lucide, intéressé par tout mais passionné uniquement par les dimensions philosophiques fondamentales de notre existence sur la planète Terre. Je suis peu intéressé par la politique quotidienne, et je n'ai jamais été un partisan ordinaire de parti politique, ni à gauche ni à droite. Je ne connais à peine les noms de vos ministres. Evidemment je vous admire énormément. Je suis un passionné de la science... sans être pour autant un grand diplômé des facultés. Au contraire. Vous verrez vite tout ça. A très bientôt. William Skyvington

Validation n° 8 — le 13 juillet 2017

Monsieur le Président : Prière de me téléphoner. Je vous expliquerai que je suis l'individu qui était responsable de la vente de sous-marins français à l'Australie. J'ai envoyé cette information déjà au premier ministre ainsi qu'à plusieurs ministères. Prière de me croire.

Validation n° 9 — le 13 juillet 2017

Monsieur le Président,

Je suis réellement l'homme qui a fait acheter des sous-marins français par l'Australie.

Ouvrez mon blog à l'adresse http://skyvington.blogspot.fr/ et utilisez le mot-clef "submarines".

Cordialement,

William Skyvington

Validation n° 10 — le 13 juillet 2017

Monsieur le Président,

Je suis réellement l'homme qui a fait acheter des sous-marins français par l'Australie.

Ouvrez mon blog à l'adresse http://skyvington.blogspot.fr/ et utilisez le mot-clef "submarines".

Cordialement,

William Skyvington

Validation n° 11 — le 13 juillet 2017

Monsieur le Président,

Je ne suis pas un dingue (pour emprunter le mot que ma fille vient d'utiliser). Je suis réellement l'homme qui a fait acheter des sous-marins français par l'Australie.

Ouvrez mon blog à l'adresse http://skyvington.blogspot.fr/ et utilisez le mot-clef "submarines".

Cordialement,

William Skyvington

Validation n° 12 — le 15 juillet 2017

Comment j'ai vendu des sous-marins à partir de ma vieille maison rurale en France

La vente de sous-marins exige, je suppose, énormément d'opérations complexes. Les spécialistes dans ce domaine doivent se donner beaucoup de mal afin de bien connaître leurs produits et de les présenter aux acheteurs potentiels à travers le monde. Quant à moi, je me suis assis tout simplement devant mon Macintosh, où je me suis servi de mon blog Antipodes comme dispositif commercial. Mes efforts étaient tout de même payants : quelques dizaines de milliards de dollars !

Toute l'histoire de cette réussite extraordinaire est contenue dans cinq articles de mon blog.

Mon premier article, du 26 décembre 2007, se retrouve à l'adresse http://skyvington.blogspot.fr/2007/12/australias-submarines.html. Dès le début, mon ton était sarcastique, parce que j'ai trouvé qu'un certain Ross Babbage parlait de sous-marins à la manière de Jules Verne. J'ai même osé dire que mon pays natal adoptait une attitude naïve envers la défense, comme s'il s'agissait d'opérations trop coûteuses pour cette nation propriétaire de quelques gisements fabuleux de richesses. Et j'ai fini par conclure que l'Australie était politiquement immature.

Dans mon second article, du 27 décembre 2007, à l'adresse http://skyvington.blogspot.fr/2007/12/nuclear-energy.html, j'ai abordé brièvement la possibilité improbable que l'Australie puisse envisager l'idée de vaisseaux à propulsion nucléaire.

Mon troisième article, du 2 janvier 2008, à l'adresse http://skyvington.blogspot.fr/2008/01/australian-arithmetic.html, restait critique des calculs financiers faits apparemment par l'Australie. Pour la première fois, j'ai suggéré explicitement que mon pays natal devrait examiner l'offre française dans ce domaine.

Mon quatrième article, du 21 janvier 2008, à l'adresse http://skyvington.blogspot.fr/2008/01/expensive-aesthetic-and-nasty.html, a commencé par une anecdore amusante concernant le Dalaï Lama. Puis j'ai retrouvé la question de chiffres financiers. En deux mots, l'Australie donnait l'impression d'envisager la dépense de beaucoup d'argent pour acheter trop peu. Mes connaissances de la situation avaient été améliorées grâce à ma lecture d'un document Kokoda envoyé par Ross Babbage. A mes yeux de débutant, ça ne collait toujours pas.

Beaucoup plus tard, mon cinquième article, du 22 avril 2016, à l'adresse http://skyvington.blogspot.fr/2016/04/did-australia-take-notice-of-my-advice.html, fut une réaction aux rumeurs selon lesquelles l'Australie aurait effectivement pris au sérieux mes conseils de vendeur naïf de sous-marins. Le 26 avril, un copain d'école, Bruce Hudson, m'a informé que l'Australie avait effectivement adopté mes suggestions en faveur de sous-marins français. Ce jour-là, la planète entière a entendu le premier ministre Malcolm Turnbull annoncer la signature d'un contrat avec le géant français DCNS pour la construction de 12 sous-marins au prix de 50 milliards de dollars australiens.

L'histoire de mon blog s'arrête là… mais celle des sous-marins ne débute qu'à peine en Australie. Curieusement, malgré tous mes efforts destinés à me faire reconnaître comme un tout petit représentant commercial dans la vente de sous-marins, personne ne m'a jamais écouté. J'ai même l'impression que les professionnels dans ce domaine évitent simplement l'emploi de l'Internet. Seraient-ils trop immergés dans les profondeurs lugubres de l'océan ?

Validation n° 13 — le 15 juillet 2017

Monsieur le Président,

Pourquoi fallait-il plus de deux ans pour que je puisse annoncer clairement le dénouement de mon rôle de "vendeur de sous-marins" ? La raison en est simple : Je comptais naïvement sur l'aide de monsieur Ross Babbage, chef de la Fondation Kokoda (dont j'ai gardé tous nos échanges de courriels). Hélas, je crains maintenant que cet individu d'origine anglaise n'était pas du tout favorable au choix de la France comme fournisseur. Aujourd'hui, il a mis totalement fin à tous ses contacts avec moi, ce qui suggère qu'il s'agissait d'une sorte de faux jeton.

Je vous prie de m'excuser de vous imposer, monsieur le Président, ces informations anecdotiques qui ne concernent que moi-même et Babbage. Quant au gouvernement australien, je n'ai jamais pu entrer en contact, à aucun moment, avec qui que ce soit.

Cordialement,

William Skyvington

Validation n° 14 — le 21 juillet 2017

Monsieur le Président,

Il est vendredi, 13 h 45, et je n'ai toujours pas reçu la moindre réaction, ni au message que je vous ai envoyé le mardi 11 juillet 2017, ni à la lettre que je vous ai écrite et mise à la poste le mercredi 19 juillet 2017. Je commence à avoir de graves doutes sur la qualité des communications de l'Elysée.

Cordialement,

William Skyvington

Validation n° 15 — le 21 juillet 2017

Monsieur le Président,

Il est vendredi, 13 h 45, et je n'ai toujours pas reçu la moindre réaction, ni au message que je vous ai envoyé le mardi 11 juillet 2017, ni à la lettre que je vous ai écrite et mise à la poste le mercredi 19 juillet 2017. Je commence à avoir de graves doutes sur la qualité des communications de l'Elysée.

Cordialement,

William Skyvington

Validation n° 16 — le 21 juillet 2017

Monsieur le Président,

J'ai de plus en plus l'impression que vous êtes totalement injoignable...

Cordialement,

William Skyvington

Validation n° 17 — le 21 juillet 2017

Monsieur le Président,

On vient de me dire au numéro 01 41 92 81 00 que je devrais attendre à peu près un mois avant de recevoir une réponse...

Eh bien, je vais attendre. Mais je suis profondément choqué par la mauvaise qualité des communications avec l'Elysée.

Cordialement,

William Skyvington

Barracuda